34

Just Add One Chinese Sister

by Patricia McMahon
and Conor Clarke McCarthy

Illustrated by Karen A. Jerome

BOYDS MILLS PRESS

Author's note

*Not so long ago, in the United States there were three people: a mother,
a father, and their son, Conor. They were happy and lucky, with a good life.
Yet something seemed to be missing.
On the other side of the world, in the city of Kunming, China, there lived
a little girl named Guan Yu. She lived with many people in a home for children.
There were other children to play with and adults to care for them,
but Guan Yu did not have a family of her own.
One day, the three people from the United States went to China to meet the
girl called Guan Yu. Although she was not at all sure about them, they knew
they wanted her to come home with them and be part of their family. . . .*

Text copyright © 2005 by Patricia McMahon and Conor Clarke McCarthy
Illustrations copyright © 2005 by Karen A. Jerome
Child's drawing on page 32 by Claire Guan Yu Gannon McCarthy

Boyds Mills Press, Inc.
A Highlights Company
815 Church Street
Honesdale, Pennsylvania 18431
Printed in China

Publisher Cataloging-in-Publication Data (U.S.)

McMahon, Patricia.
Just add one Chinese sister / by Patricia McMahon ;
and Conor Clarke McCarthy / illustrated by Karen A. Jerome.—1st ed.
p. : ill. ; cm.
ISBN 1-56397-989-6
1. Adopted children — United States — Juvenile literature. 2. Chinese American children — Juvenile literature.
3. Intercountry adoption — United States — Juvenile literature. 4. Intercountry adoption — China — Juvenile literature.
5. Brothers and sisters — Juvenile literature. I. McCarthy, Conor Clarke. II. Jerome, Karen A. III. Title.
362.73/4 E dc22   HV875.55M36 2005

First edition, 2005
Book design by Amy Drinker, Aster Designs
The text of this book is set in 15.5-point Minion.
10 9 8 7 6 5 4 3 2 1

For my sister, Claire, the bravest person I know
—C. C. M.

For the daughters of China, most especially my own,
and for those of us who love them, both here and there
—P. M.

To Kathy, Don, Laura, and Pedro Magni,
for all their support over the years
—K. J.

Hey, big girl, would you like to help me?

I'm putting all these pictures in a book.

Here's one of a very sleepy guy.

And look, this is a picture of a worried little girl.

You want me to tell you her story again?

Good—that's just what I'm about to do.

Here is a picture of three people walking a dog.

I know you know them.

Why do I have a sock?

Because it's going into the book.

Why am I doing this? Because these are all parts

of my favorite story—the one about you.

The picture with the dog, let's put that first.

Yes, that is me, Daddy, your brother,

and Rosie—Rosie the Wonder Dog.

Conor is not a brother in this picture. Not yet.

He needs a sister before he can become a brother.

Mom announced today that
we are going to adopt a
little girl. From China, no less.
What do I think? she wonders.
I need a sister, she says.
I should be a brother.
Truth is, I wouldn't mind.
Only how do I become a brother?

Why don't we add
some words Conor wrote?
He thought a lot about you
before you came home with us.

Hand me the card with the pretty flower on it.

It says CONGRATULATIONS.

It means that all our papers have gone to China,

and we should be happy.

Soon we will hear about a little girl who will be our little girl.

Why this silly picture of me with a big pile of paper?

Daddy and Conor thought it looked funny.

What was it for? For you—

Five Things I Wonder
About Being a Brother:
1) Will she like me?
2) Will she annoy me?
3) Will I have to lock my room?
4) Will she get dibs on the TV?
5) Will she like sports?

so the people in China would
know we were a family who could
take good care of a little girl.
Maybe Conor's list should go here.

Now this picture—
a worried-looking little girl named Guan Yu.
This is the first time we ever saw your face.
I was so happy to have a daughter that I cried.
Daddy said, "There's our girl." Conor put his
hands in the air and said, "Yes!"

*Big news. A lady from the
adoption agency called to say
she was sending us an e-mail
with a picture. We crowded
around the computer. Slowly
a picture filled the screen.
A short-haired, worried-looking
little girl stared out at us.
We stared back.
I have a sister.*

Later, I went outside to see the stars.
I thought, *These are the same stars
that are over my little girl's bed in
China.* I made a wish that you
were all right.

This invitation can go here.
There was a party before we
left to find you. All our friends
wanted to celebrate with us.
They gave you dresses, dolls,

I think this new sister now
has more clothing than I do.
And more toys than I had.
Hmmm. And what about
all this pink frilly stuff?
I was hoping for
a tree-climbing,
hockey-playing sister.
This is worrisome.
We leave soon.
Dad keeps packing and
unpacking the suitcases.
We still have too much stuff.

a tutu to dance in, an easel
to paint on—so many things.
Yes, it was the pink tutu.
I know, you do like to dance.

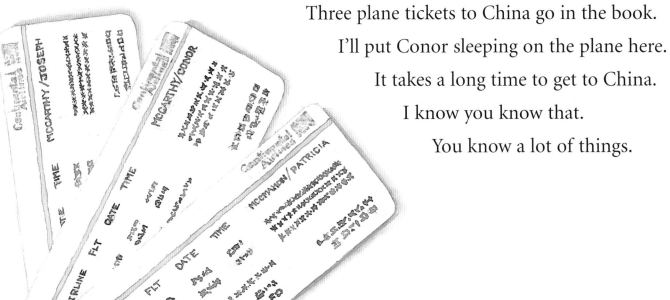

Three plane tickets to China go in the book.

I'll put Conor sleeping on the plane here.

It takes a long time to get to China.

I know you know that.

You know a lot of things.

*Finally, we are on our way
to China. First, we will spend
a week in Beijing for—
surprise!—more papers.
Then on to Kunming where
I get to meet my sister!
We have decided to add
"Claire" to her name. It was
my idea—Claire Guan Yu.
Next we go to the city of
Guangzhou for the papers we
need to bring Claire home.
And then back to Beijing.*

Now this picture of a very sad little
girl. Yes, it's you! Do you know
when this was? It was when we first
met. Lots of people were in a room
waiting to meet their babies.
A woman handed you to me and said,
"Here is your mommy."
I hugged you. Daddy stood very close.
Conor put his hand on your back.
You looked at us. And then you
started screaming. A big scream.
Don't laugh, you did. A big
"Get-me-out-of-here!" scream.
That's right, you didn't know us.
How could you like us,
if you didn't know us?
But we were ready
to like you.
I already
loved you,
I think.
Except when
you kicked me!
Yes, you did.

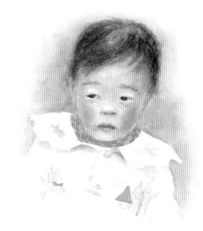

Tomorrow is my birthday,
but who cares? Today we
got Claire. She is so pretty
and so scared. She reminds me
of that line from the spooky
movies, "It's quiet, too quiet."
Mom said this might happen.
I mean, we don't even
speak the same language.
But still, it's frustrating.

We have lots of pictures of our new family in Kunming. You and Daddy on the merry-go-round, and the tickets. Daddy and Conor playing badminton—anywhere they could find space! You would chase the shuttle for them. Look at these three ladies. They are old, old women.

Aren't they beautiful?

They stopped me to ask questions.

Would you go home with us?

Where would you sleep?

Would you go to school?

Questions, questions, questions.

I answered all I could. I told them

I would help you to be anything

you wanted to be. No, I didn't say

a gymnast. I didn't know that yet.

*I have discovered my mom
talks to people even when she
cannot speak their language.
Our poor translator is always
running after her trying to see
what she is doing. Today,
my mom was telling these three
ancient women, half in English,
half in Chinese, all the
amazing things Claire is
going to do with her life.
And the oldest one—I am not
kidding, this woman was about
102 years old—she looked hard
at my mother. Then she
looked hard at Claire. Then
she nodded her head and gave
my mom a thumbs up. So cool!*

White Swan
Hotel
Guangzhou

Let's add this postcard of our hotel in
Guangzhou. And the sock, too.
Why? Because in this story,
it is a famous sock.
Conor made a football out of socks
so he could play in the hotel.
Sometimes you and Conor had to
wait while we looked at papers, or
checked computers, or talked on the
phone. So boring.
Conor invented Hotel Ball, which he
would play with Daddy. Or by himself.
He tried to play with you. But you just
stared at him—as if he were a strange
person. You never smiled.
Should I read you Conor's words?

*Today will forever stand
etched in my memory.
I got my first laugh out of Claire.
Dad and I were playing catch
with my sock football.
He threw it over my head
onto the bed next to where Claire
stood watching us.
I yelled "Fumble!" and dove for it.
The next thing we knew,
Claire was laughing her head off.
It was the sweetest sound.
It sounded as if that laugh
had been trapped inside her,
and finally burst out.*

Once you started laughing, you kept going. Laughing and laughing. Loudly.

We thought it was wonderful. Except for the time we gave you ice cream.

I know you like ice cream. But this ice cream made you so silly.

You were running, shouting, bouncing off the walls.

Daddy and Conor tried to catch you.

We looked like we were making a funny movie.

I had this great idea to take Claire swimming. She took one look at the pool and began to cry. I jumped in to show her what fun it was. That made her yell even louder. Cry! Scream! Howl! Dad said maybe Claire thought the pool was eating me.

This is the spoon from the ice cream. And this is a bill for a bathing suit that I paid too much money for, so you could swim in the hotel pool with Conor. But you didn't, did you?

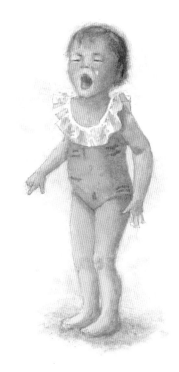

Here's a picture of you and Conor,

back in Beijing on our last day in China.

Yes, it was snowing. And it was Thanksgiving Day.

I kept thinking that this was your last day in your first home.

I was hoping you would like your new home.

I want to remember everything
so I can tell Claire in case she
doesn't remember China.
Everything here is so different.
The streets are jammed with
people. So many bicycles
lined up, sharing the roads
with cars. The smell—a
more raw, damp smell.
The hills surrounding Kunming.
The small, small restaurants
with wonderful food.
This is Claire's other home.
I respect it.

I was amazed at how our new family
felt exactly right.
At how much I loved you already.
At how glad I was you had stopped
kicking me.

Now there are four airplane tickets, one for each member of our family. All the people in this picture were waiting to meet you.

*Claire became scared
and shy again with
all the new people.
Easy does it, I thought.
My sister has to
get to know you.
I held her hand.*

The airport was filled with friends
and family, holding big balloons and
a sign saying WELCOME HOME.
It was good to see them.

Now here are some pictures
of our family back at home.
You and Conor and Daddy
trick-or-treating. And the time
you painted Rosie. . . .

*Well, the shy, scared sister
has disappeared. Sometimes
when I hear little kids
running around our house,
or Claire singing
"Old MacDonald" loudly in
her fast-learned English,
I wonder if this
disappearance is a
good thing. But then Claire's
laughter always tells me
that it is.*

You had to have a time-out.
Yup, you were angry.
And Rosie was red, blue,
and yellow.

Here Rosie looks worried, not you!

Can you count how many dolls are on her back?

One, two, three, four, five—that's right. And your panda.

She likes to have dolls on her back? She told you that?

OK, I believe you.

Someone asked Claire today,
"Is that your brother?"
She said, "Can't you tell?"
That was perfect.
She is almost perfect.
Except she does get dibs
on the TV. Which is not fair.
And I do have a sign on my room:

I have to keep moving it higher.
And she sometimes annoys me.
And she does not seem to like
sports, which is a big problem.
She does seem to like anything
pink, or with the word
"princess" on it. Hmmm.
But I do think she likes me.
And I know the answer
to my question now.
How do you become a brother?

You want to draw a picture?
That's a great idea.
I know you are a good artist.
And that will be a perfect way
to finish our book.

BY CLAIRE

. . . just add one Chinese sister.

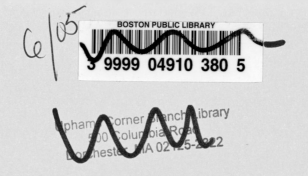